INSIDE INFO

TAKING APART THE
HUMAN BODY
... TO FIND OUT HOW IT WORKS!

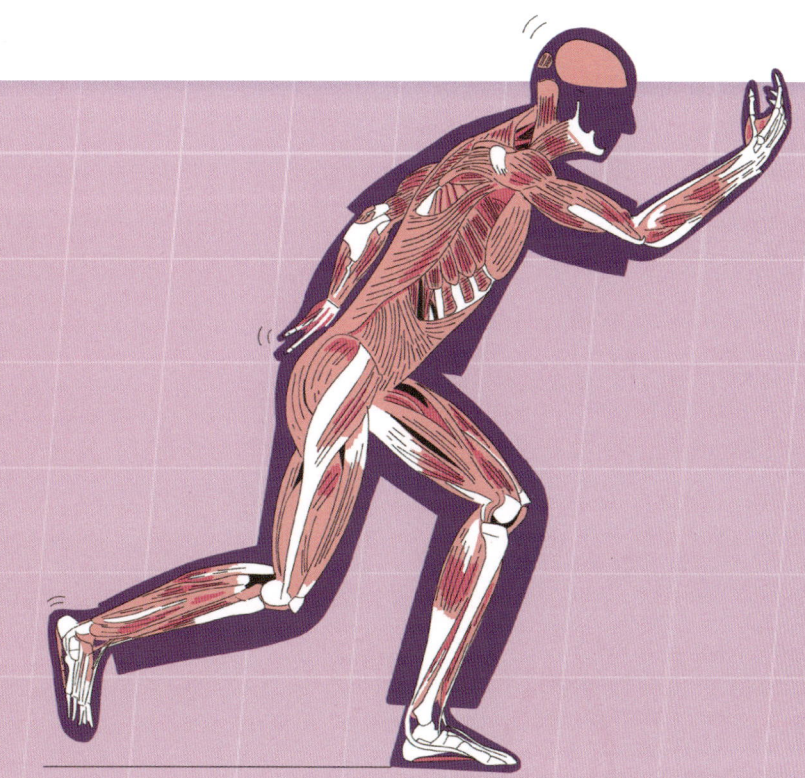

BY CHRIS OXLADE AND SEAN O'BRIEN

WAYLAND

First published in Great Britain in 2025
by Wayland
Copyright © Hodder and Stoughton, 2025

All rights reserved.

Editor: Grace Glendinning
Designer: Peter Scoulding
Illustrations: Sean O'Brien

HB ISBN: 978 1 5263 2700 0
PB ISBN: 978 1 5263 2702 4
EB ISBN: 978 1 5263 2701 7

Printed and bound in China

Wayland, an imprint of
Hachette Children's Group
Part of Hodder and Stoughton
Carmelite House
50 Victoria Embankment
London EC4Y 0DZ

An Hachette UK Company
www.hachette.co.uk
www.hachettechildrens.co.uk

The website addresses (URLs) included in this book were valid at the time of going to press. However, it is possible that contents or addresses may have changed since the publication of this book. No responsibility for any such changes can be accepted by either the author or the Publisher.

The authorised representative in the EEA is Hachette Ireland, 8 Castlecourt Centre, Castleknock Road, Castleknock, Dublin 15, D15 YF6A, Ireland

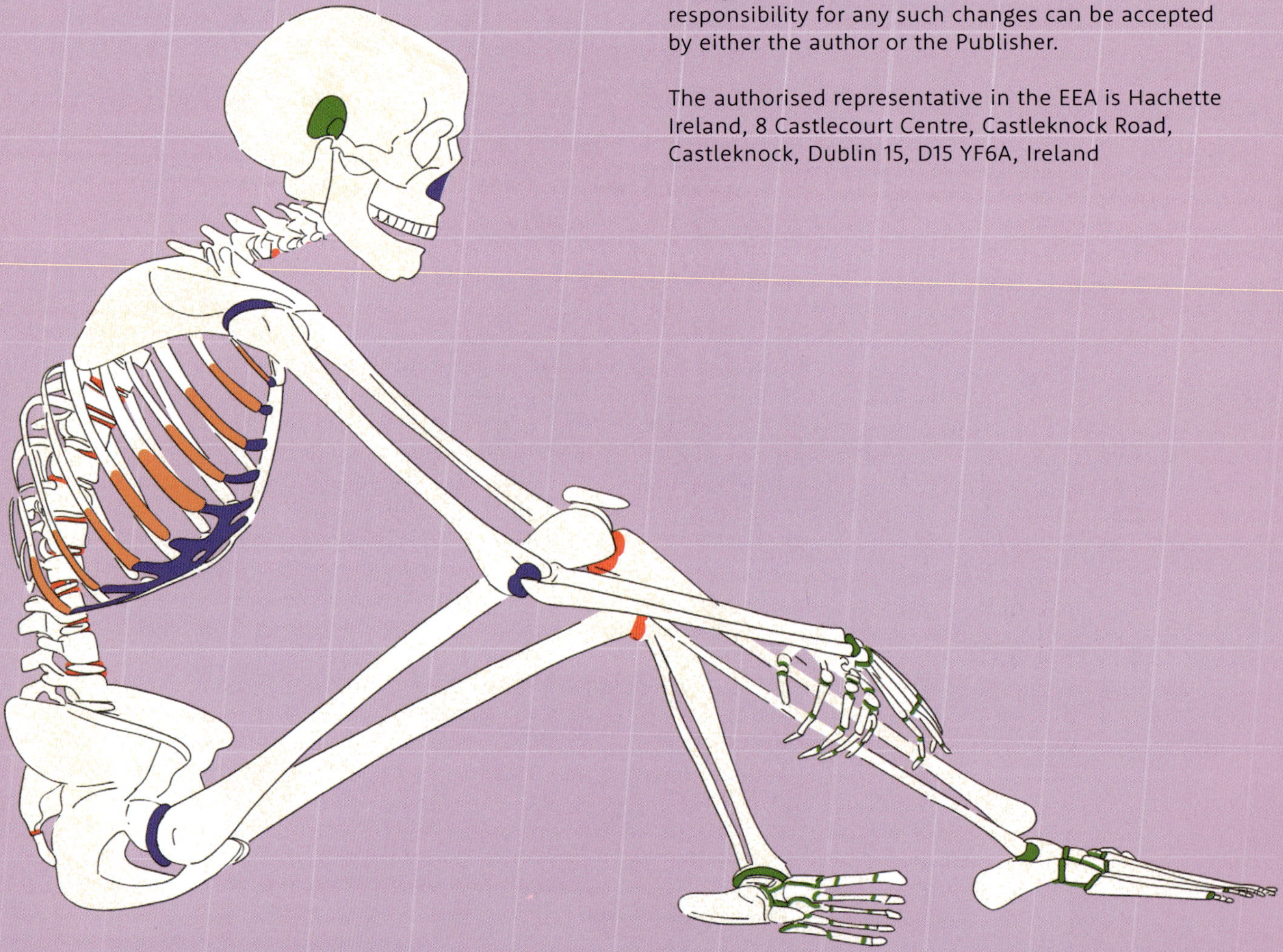

CONTENTS

Inside the Human Body	4
Our Mighty Outer Layer	6
Layers of Muscles	8
Bony Bits	10
Inside a Bone	12
Inside Your Head	14
Nerves and Senses	16
Bits About the Blood	18
Blood Pump	20
Made for Breathing	22
Dealing with Food	24
Body Building Blocks	26
A Look Inside	28
Glossary	30
Further Information	31
Index	32

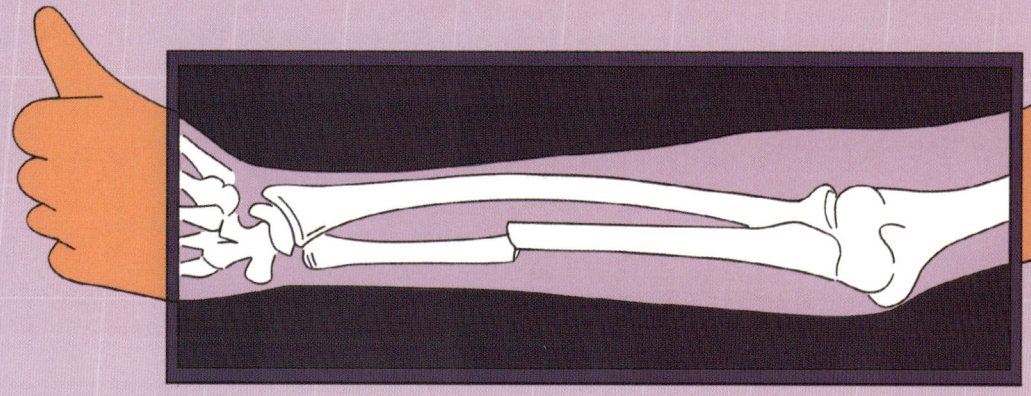

INSIDE THE HUMAN BODY

Hmmmm ...

Have you ever wondered what's inside your body? What bits and pieces are there and what do they all do? Medical students dissect (take apart) bodies as they learn to be doctors, surgeons open up patients' bodies to fix them and doctors use amazing machines to see through our skin. Now it's your turn to take a look at what makes your insides work!

In this book, we'll explore the science of all these layers, from the surface of the skin to the centre of our bones ...

Your **DIGESTIVE SYSTEM** starts in your **MOUTH** and moves down the **OESOPHAGUS** to your **STOMACH** and **INTESTINES**. It pulls out all the useful chemicals from your food.

Your **SKELETON** is a frame of bones that supports all the other parts of your body.

JOINTS in the skeleton let your skeleton bend and twist.

MUSCLES make your body move. They are attached to your bones to make your joints bend.

Your **LUNGS** are part of the **RESPIRATORY SYSTEM**, which gets oxygen into your body.

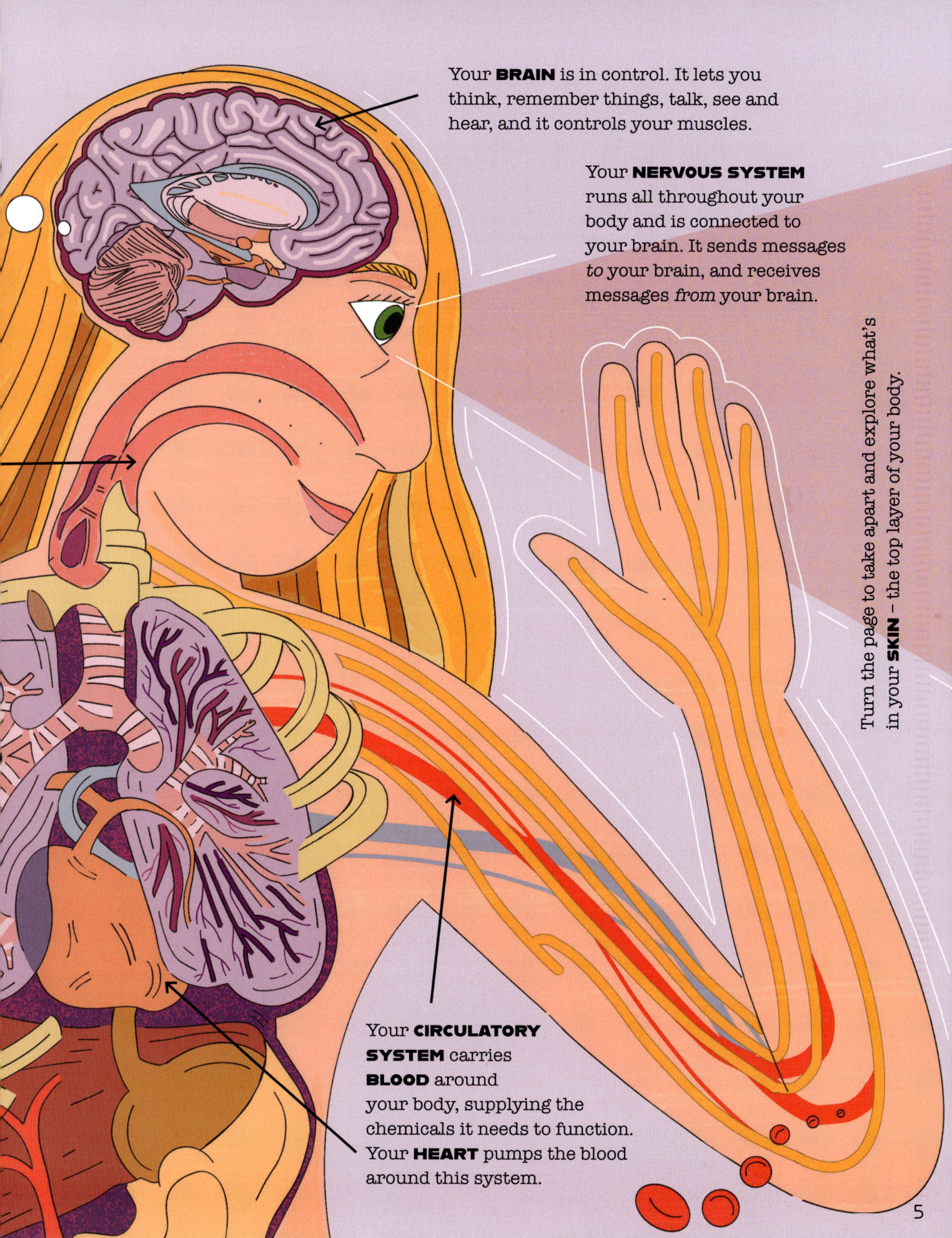

Our Mighty Outer Layer

Your skin is your body's outer layer. It's tough and waterproof, and it protects the inside your body from germs. It contains hair follicles that grow hairs and glands that make sweat to cool you down.

Going under the skin's surface we find different layers.

The skin's top layer is called the **EPIDERMIS**. It's made of dead skin cells that gradually rub off.

The **DERMIS** is the skin's lower layer. New skin cells grow here.

A **HAIR SHAFT** grows out of a follicle.

Hair **FOLLICLES** are pits in the skin from which hairs grow.

There's a layer of **FAT** under the skin.

Tiny **BLOOD VESSELS** supply the skin with blood.

ZOOM IN!

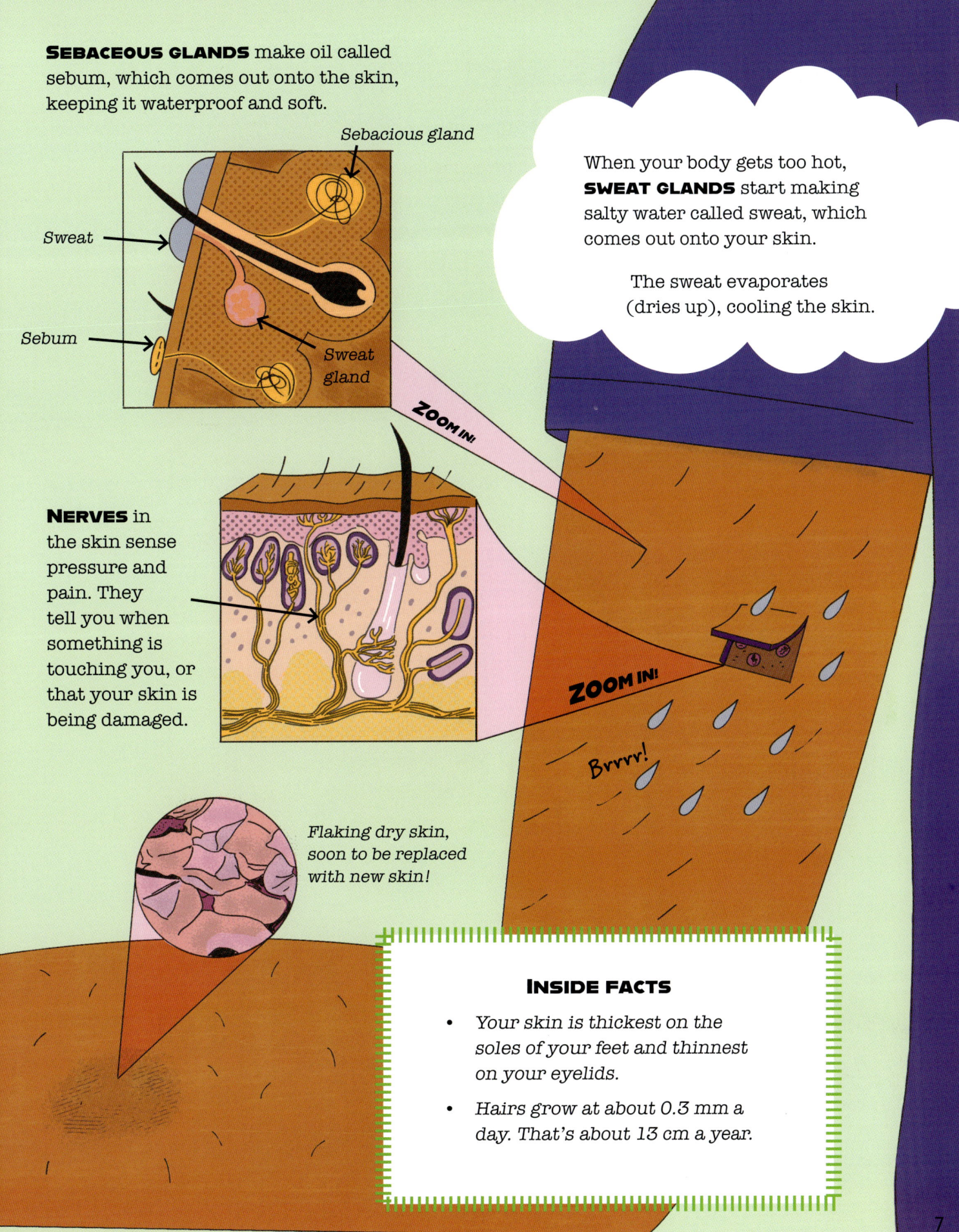

Layers of Muscles

If we look under the skin, we find a layer of muscles that covers most of your body. Muscles support your skeleton and make it move. Your brain makes your muscles contract and relax to make the joints in your skeleton bend and twist, so you can run, dance, lift stuff up and grip objects. There are about 640 muscles altogether. They make up your muscular system.

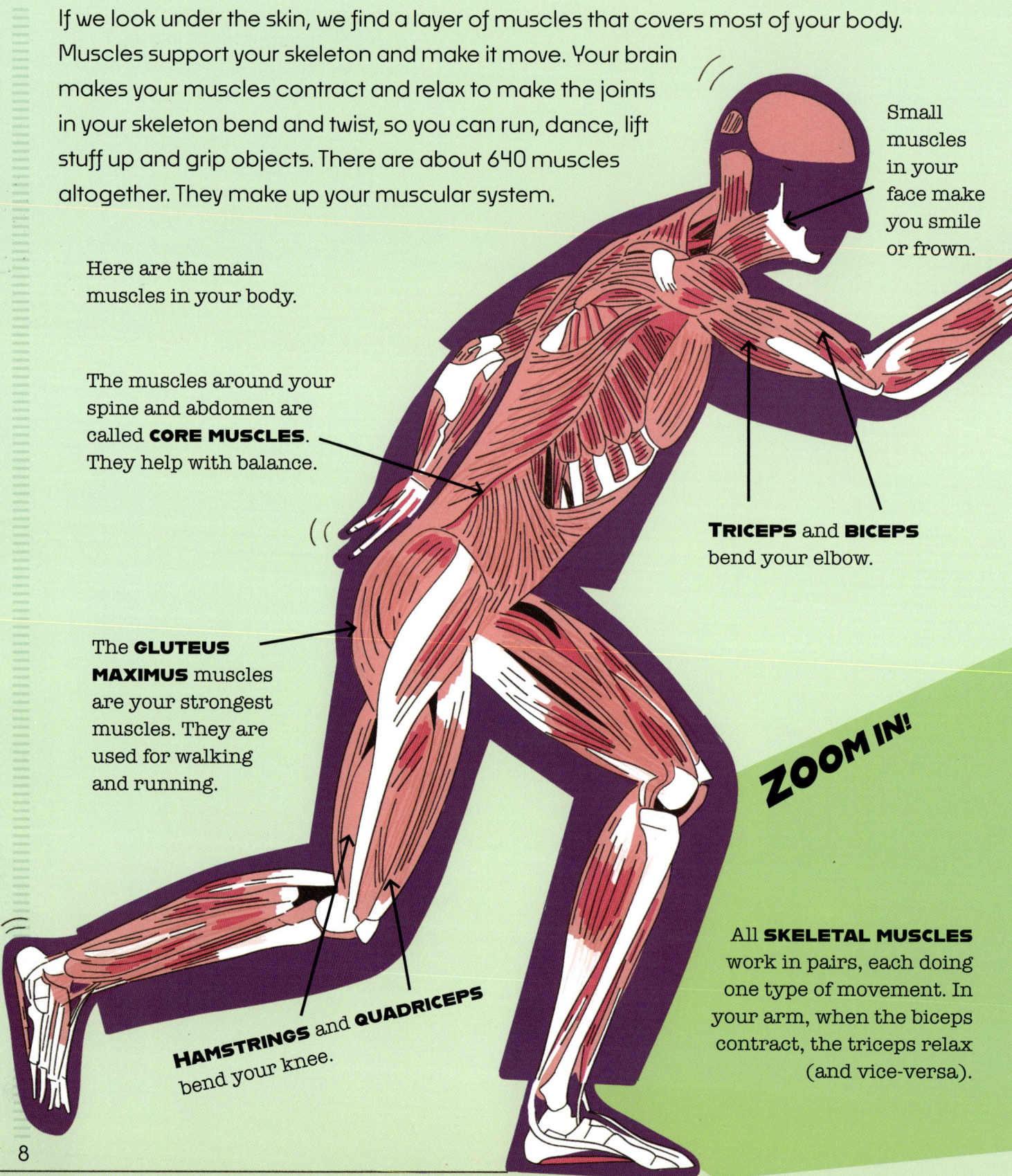

Here are the main muscles in your body.

The muscles around your spine and abdomen are called **CORE MUSCLES**. They help with balance.

The **GLUTEUS MAXIMUS** muscles are your strongest muscles. They are used for walking and running.

Small muscles in your face make you smile or frown.

TRICEPS and **BICEPS** bend your elbow.

HAMSTRINGS and **QUADRICEPS** bend your knee.

ZOOM IN!

All **SKELETAL MUSCLES** work in pairs, each doing one type of movement. In your arm, when the biceps contract, the triceps relax (and vice-versa).

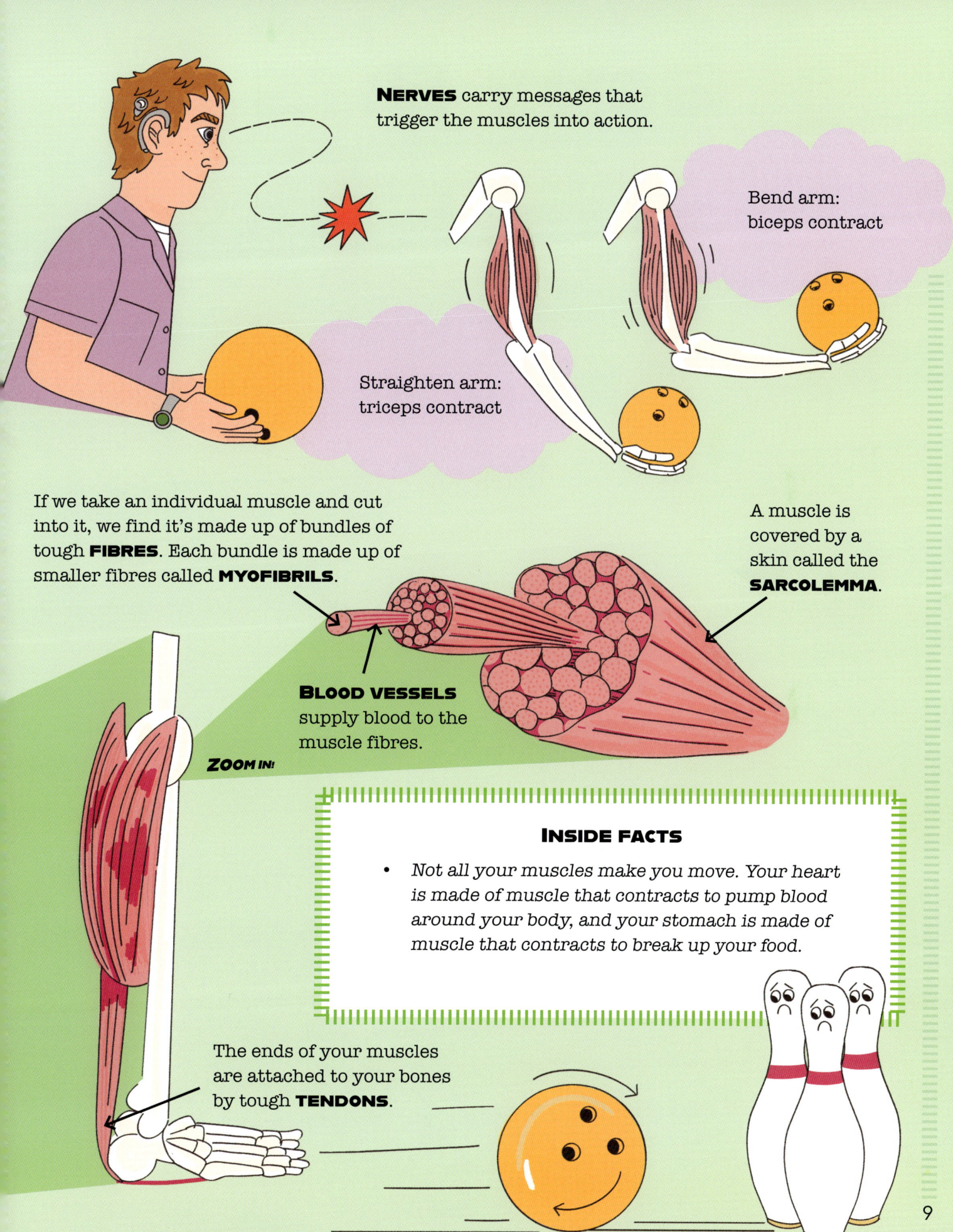

Bony Bits

Peeling back your muscles, we can see the bones of your skeleton. The skeleton is a strong frame that keeps your body in shape. Altogether, you have more than 200 bones – some very big and some very small.

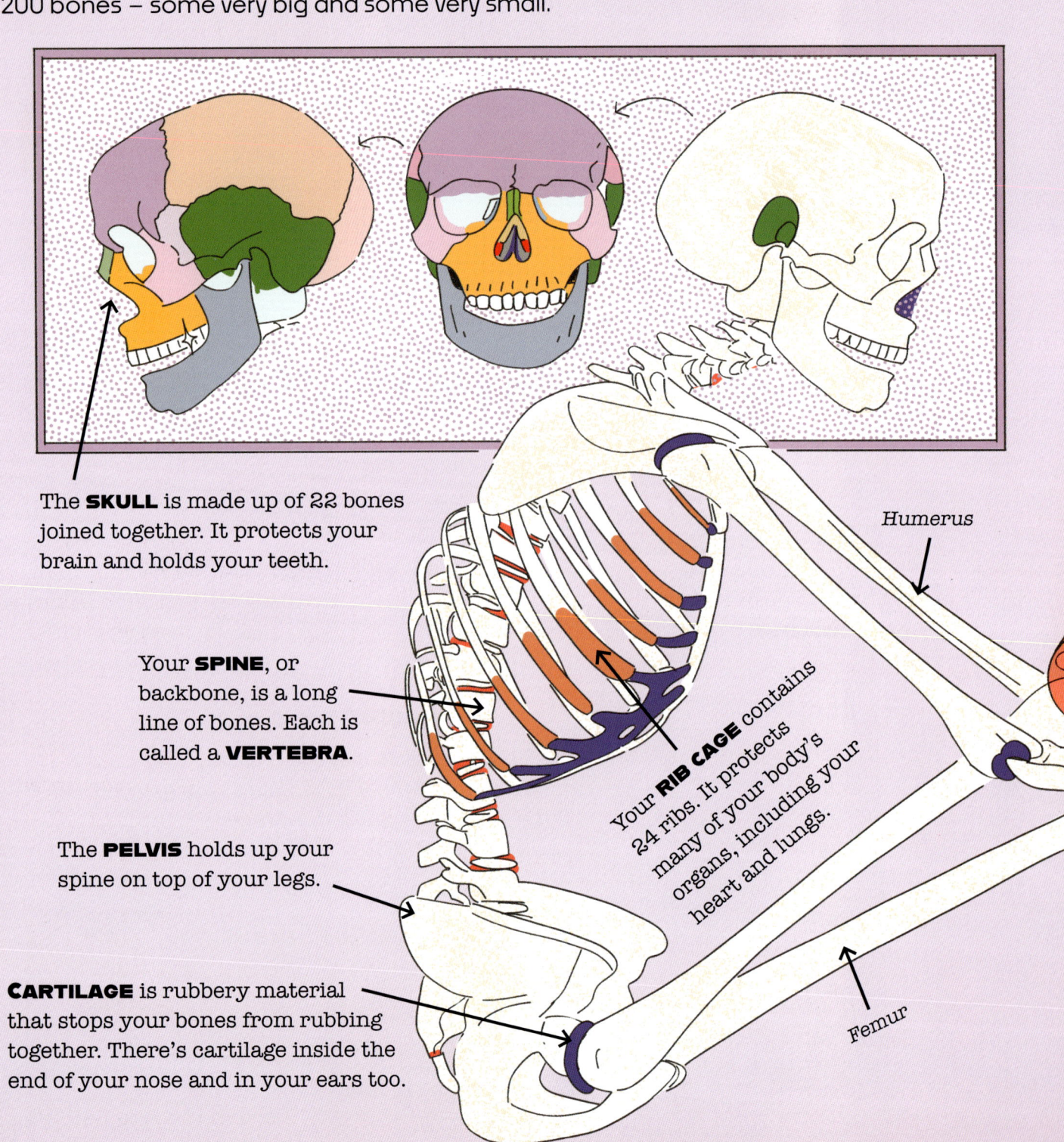

The **SKULL** is made up of 22 bones joined together. It protects your brain and holds your teeth.

Your **SPINE**, or backbone, is a long line of bones. Each is called a **VERTEBRA**.

Your **RIB CAGE** contains 24 ribs. It protects many of your body's organs, including your heart and lungs.

The **PELVIS** holds up your spine on top of your legs.

CARTILAGE is rubbery material that stops your bones from rubbing together. There's cartilage inside the end of your nose and in your ears too.

Humerus

Femur

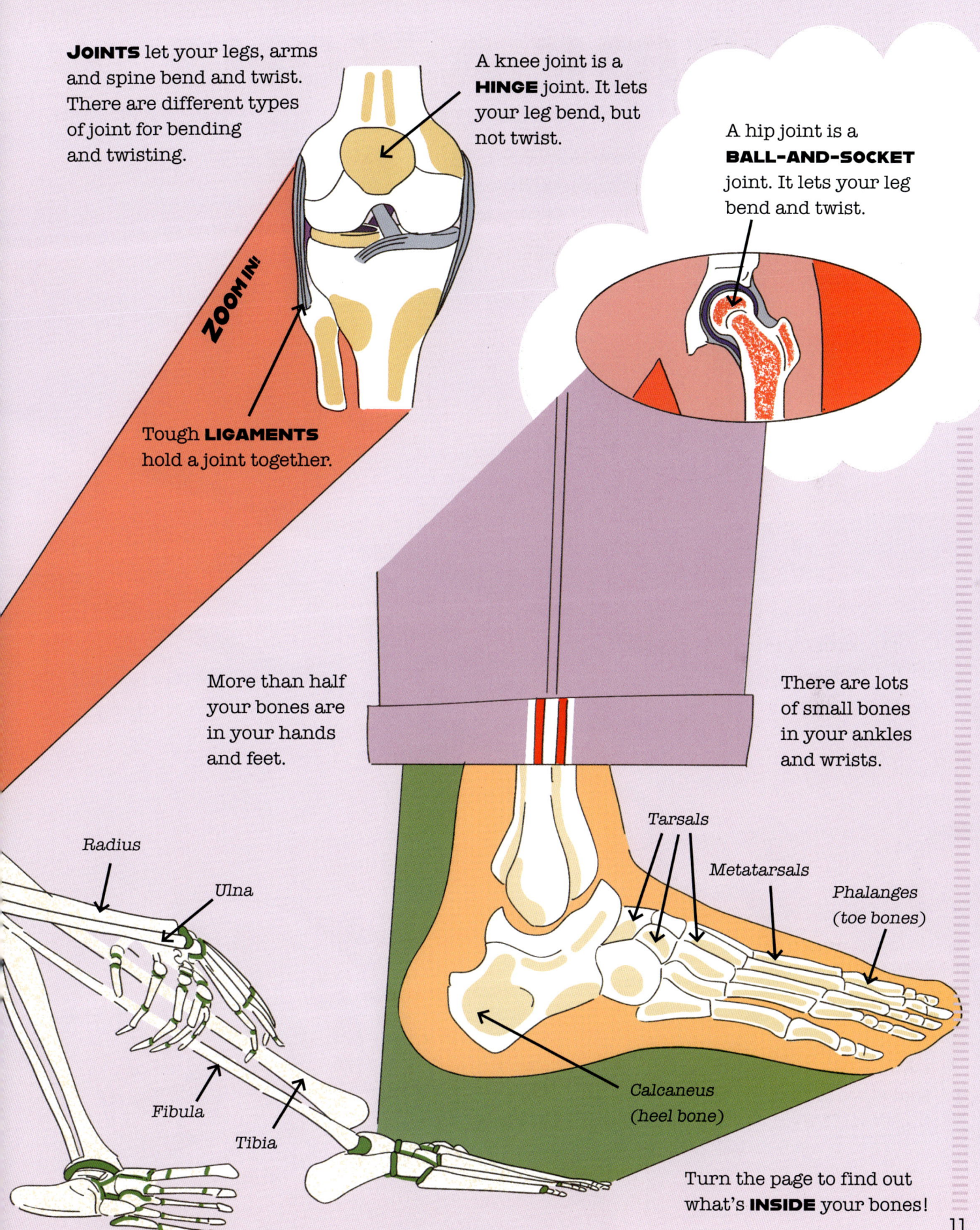

JOINTS let your legs, arms and spine bend and twist. There are different types of joint for bending and twisting.

A knee joint is a **HINGE** joint. It lets your leg bend, but not twist.

A hip joint is a **BALL-AND-SOCKET** joint. It lets your leg bend and twist.

ZOOM IN!

Tough **LIGAMENTS** hold a joint together.

More than half your bones are in your hands and feet.

There are lots of small bones in your ankles and wrists.

Tarsals

Metatarsals

Phalanges (toe bones)

Radius

Ulna

Fibula

Tibia

Calcaneus (heel bone)

Turn the page to find out what's **INSIDE** your bones!

11

INSIDE A BONE

Let's see what we find if we cut into a bone. Bones are hard on the outside but soft and spongy inside. This makes them very strong, but also flexible—and lightweight—enough for us to move around comfortably. They are made of living material – blood vessels and nerves run all through them.

Below is what the inside of a femur looks like.

The bone is covered with a membrane called the **PERIOSTEUM**. It protects the bone and helps to heal the bone if it gets damaged.

The outer layer of bone is called **COMPACT** bone. It is extremely hard and makes the bone strong.

NERVES tell your brain if the bone gets damaged.

BLOOD VESSELS supply the bone with blood.

The bone inside is full of holes called **PORES**, like a sponge. It is much softer than the outer bone.

ZOOM IN!

In the femur, the sponge is formed by bunches of strands called **TRABECULAE**.

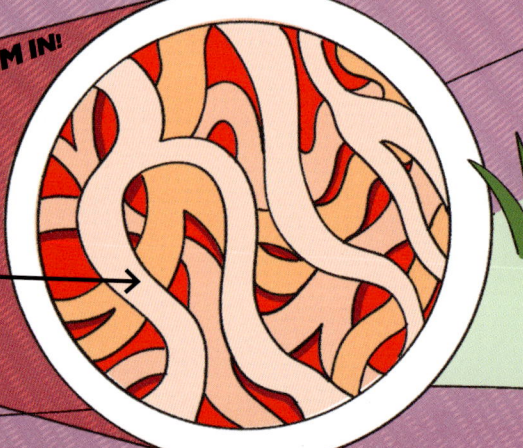

The spongy bone at each end of a femur is filled with jelly-like red material called **MARROW**. This works as a **RED BLOOD CELL** factory, supplying the body with fresh cells to replace dead ones.

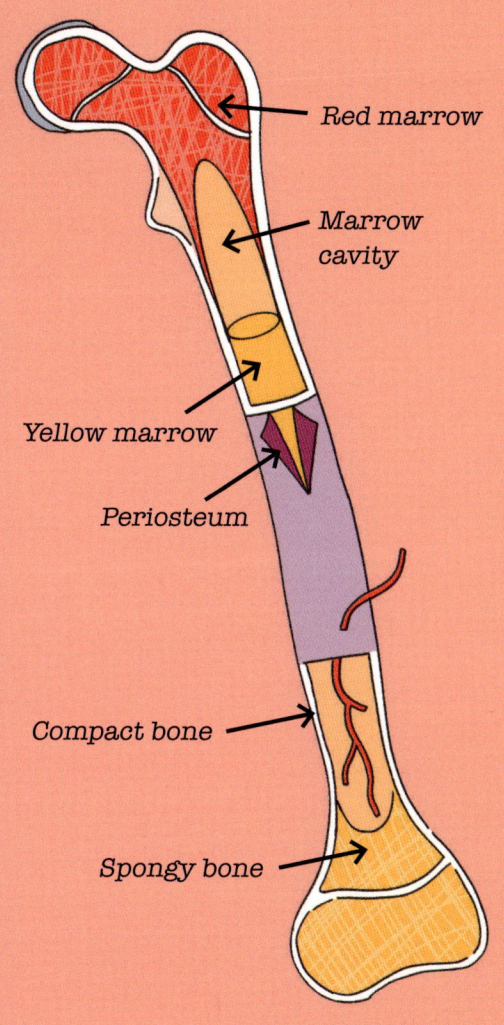

- Red marrow
- Marrow cavity
- Yellow marrow
- Periosteum
- Compact bone
- Spongy bone

Long bones like the femur have a cavity in the middle that's filled with fat-storing **YELLOW MARROW**, too.

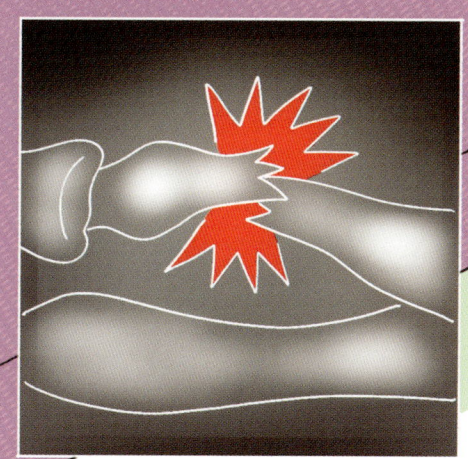

Bones are springy and tough, but they can break if they are bent too much. New bone grows to fix the repair.

I'm glad I don't have bones. Ouch!

INSIDE YOUR HEAD

If we open up your skull, we find your brain inside! Also inside your head are spaces for your eyes and ears, teeth in your jaws, and passages that connect your nose and mouth.

The brain in your head is the most complicated organ in your body.

It's made up of about 100 billion brain cells, called **NEURONS**, connected to each other in a complicated network. It's the main part of the nervous system.

Different areas of your brain do different jobs. Here are some of the key areas:

The **CEREBRAL CORTEX** is the outer layer of the brain, and it controls your senses, your movement and your emotions.

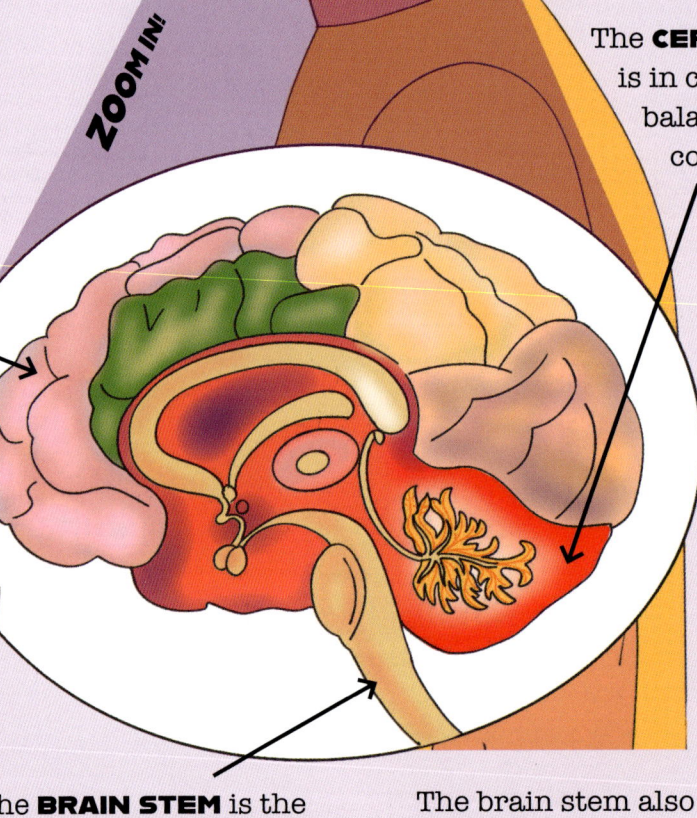

The **CEREBELLUM** is in charge of balance and co-ordination.

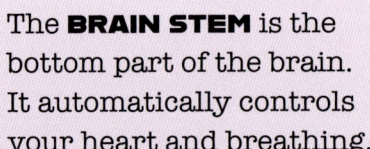

The **BRAIN STEM** is the bottom part of the brain. It automatically controls your heart and breathing.

The brain stem also connects to the spinal cord, which connects to the rest of your nervous system (see pages 16–17).

Your **NOSTRILS** are connected by passages to the back of your throat.

The **EPIGLOTTIS** is a flap that stops food going into lungs when you swallow.

Your **TONGUE** is a muscle attached to the base of your mouth.

VOCAL CORDS vibrate to make sound when you talk.

Your **TEETH** are held firmly in place in your **JAW**. As you grow, your first set of teeth are replaced by adult teeth.

Upper jaw

Lower jaw

Adult teeth waiting to come through.

INSIDE FACTS
- An adult brain weighs about 1.4 kg (3 lbs).

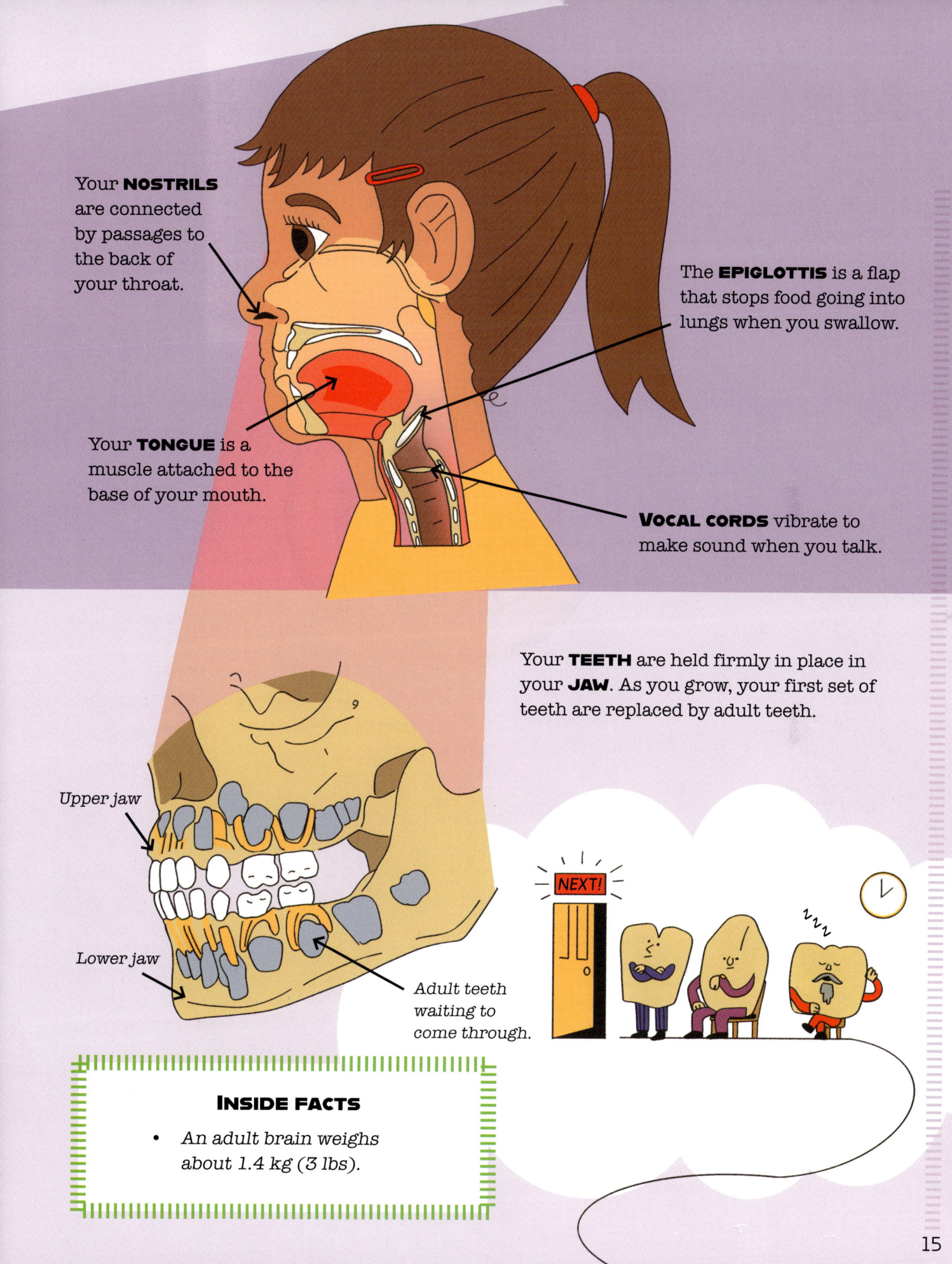

Nerves and Senses

Nerves start from your brain and reach almost every part of your body. When you feel a thorn pricking your finger, your nerves are at work. They send messages from your brain to your body and from your body to your brain. Your senses (touch, sight, hearing, smell and taste) all use nerves to send messages to your brain.

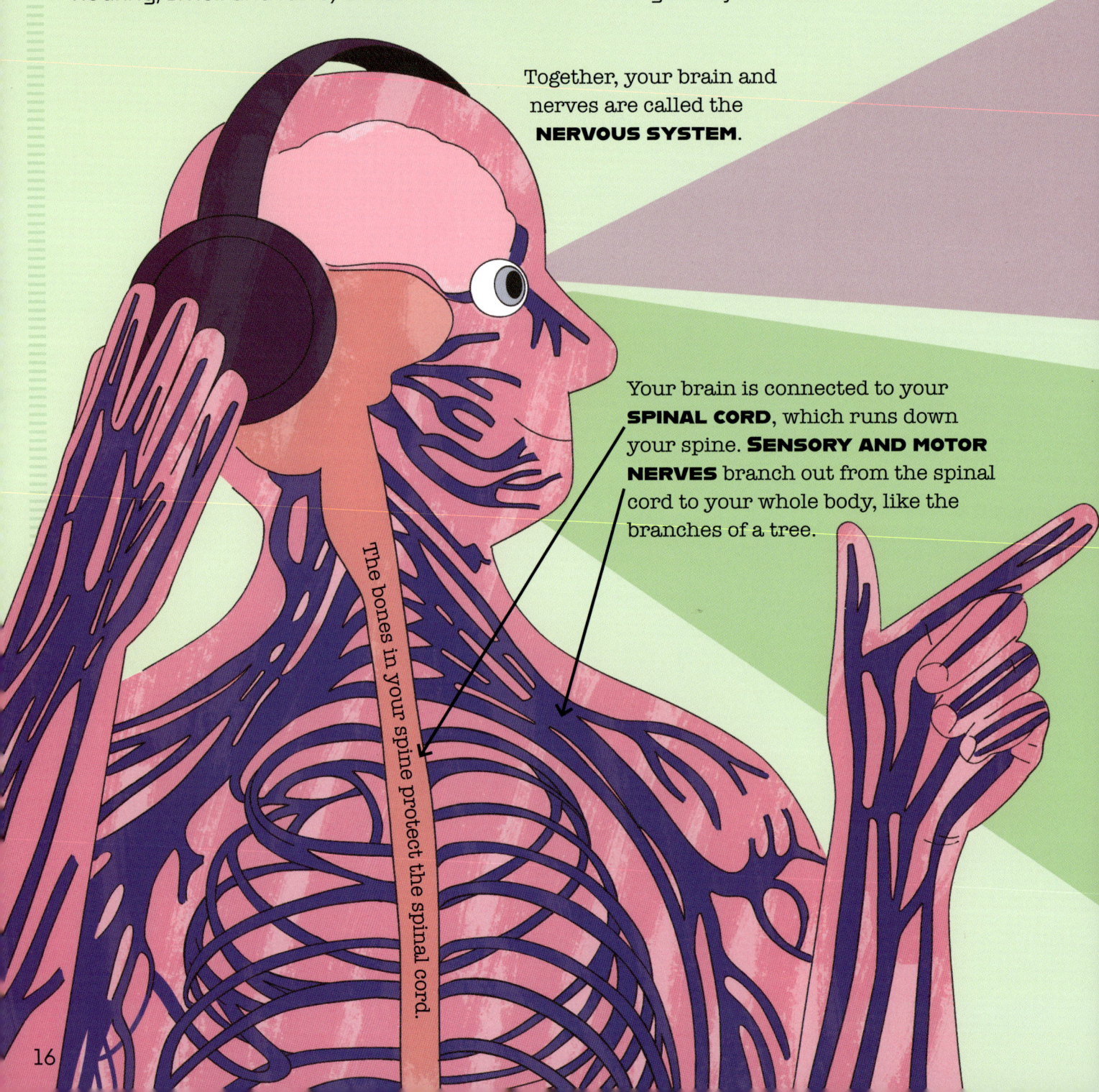

Together, your brain and nerves are called the **NERVOUS SYSTEM**.

Your brain is connected to your **SPINAL CORD**, which runs down your spine. **SENSORY AND MOTOR NERVES** branch out from the spinal cord to your whole body, like the branches of a tree.

The bones in your spine protect the spinal cord.

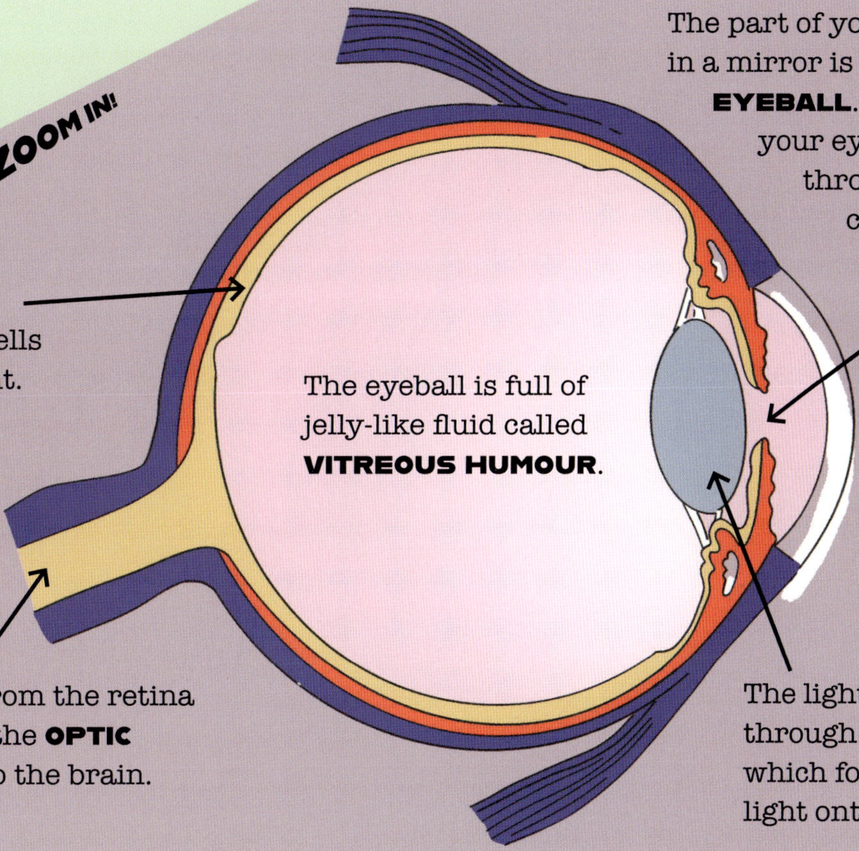

ZOOM IN!

The part of your eye you see in a mirror is the front of the **EYEBALL**. Light goes inside your eye here, first through an opening called the **PUPIL**.

The **RETINA** is covered with cells that detect light.

The eyeball is full of jelly-like fluid called **VITREOUS HUMOUR**.

Signals from the retina go along the **OPTIC NERVE** to the brain.

The light passes through a **LENS**, which focusses the light onto the retina.

Your **EAR FLAPS** on the outside of your head are only a small part of your ears. The rest is inside your head.

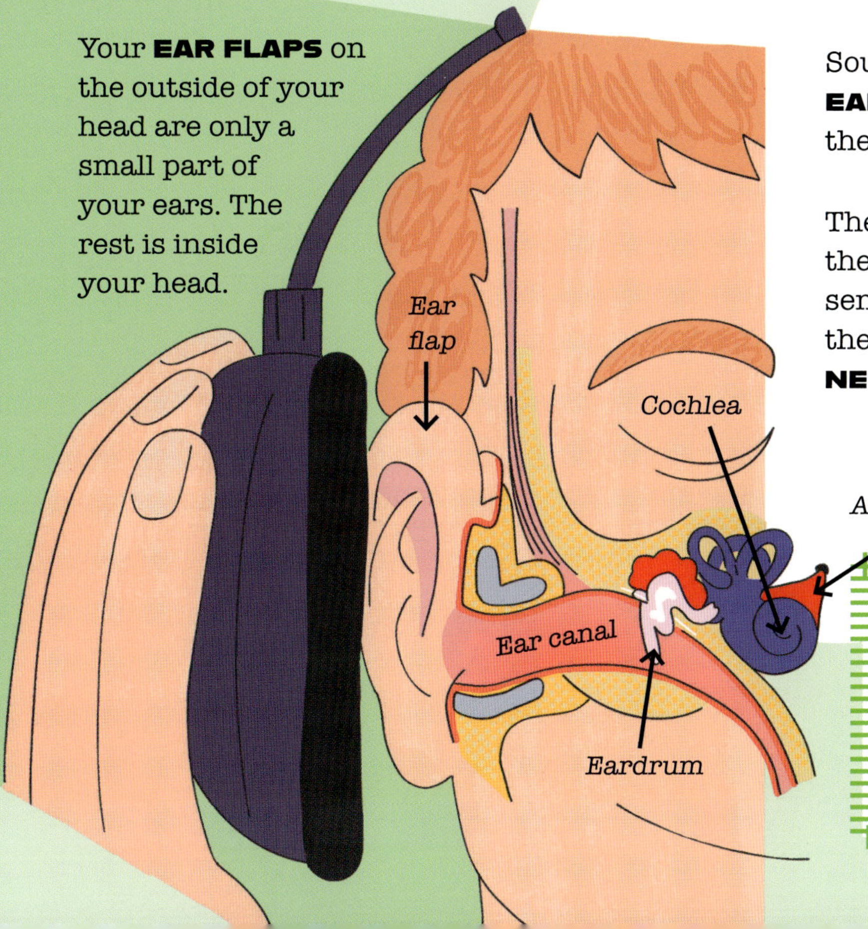

Sound goes along the **EAR CANAL** and makes the **EARDRUM** vibrate.

The **COCHLEA** detects the vibrations and sends signals along the **AUDITORY NERVE** to the brain.

Ear flap

Cochlea

Auditory nerve

Ear canal

Eardrum

INSIDE FACTS

- *The smell receptors inside your nose can detect more than 3,000 different smells.*

Bits About the Blood

All through the body we find a network of tubes called blood vessels that transport blood. When you graze a knee or prick a finger, these tubes get damaged and you see blood seeping out. Blood is your body's transport system. It carries important chemicals through your circulatory system.

Blood is pumped around by your heart (see pages 20–21).

Blood visits the lungs to collect oxygen (see pages 22–23).

Blood flows from the heart to the body, back to the heart, to the lungs, and back to the heart again.

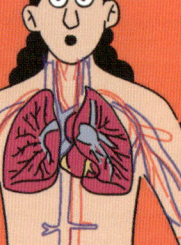

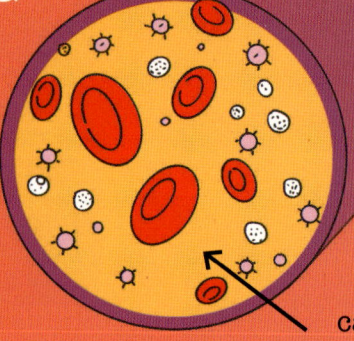

Blood contains a watery liquid called **PLASMA**. Blood cells and platelets are carried along in the plasma, and chemicals such as sugar are dissolved in the plasma.

RED BLOOD CELLS carry oxygen. They collect it in the lungs and give it to cells around your body.

PLATELETS  clot your blood, which helps to fix any leaks in blood vessels.

WHITE BLOOD CELLS fight disease. They attack germs such as bacteria and viruses.

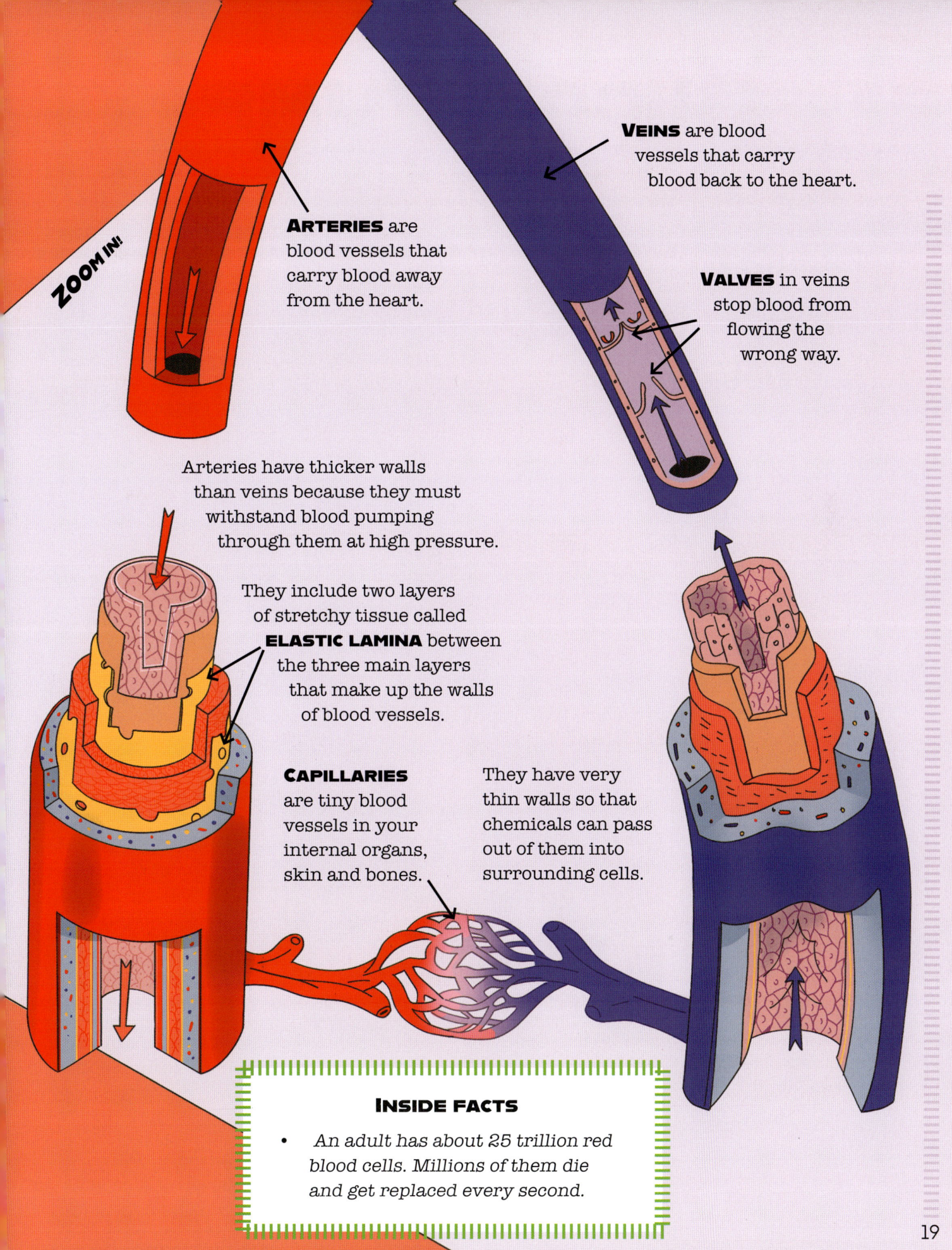

BLOOD PUMP

The thump, thump coming from your chest is your heart doing its job: pumping blood through your blood vessels. The human heart is about the size of a clenched fist and is made of cardiac muscle.

The heart has four spaces inside, called **CHAMBERS**, two on the left and two on the right.

As in veins, **VALVES** in the heart stop the blood from flowing the wrong direction. There are four different types of valve in the human heart.

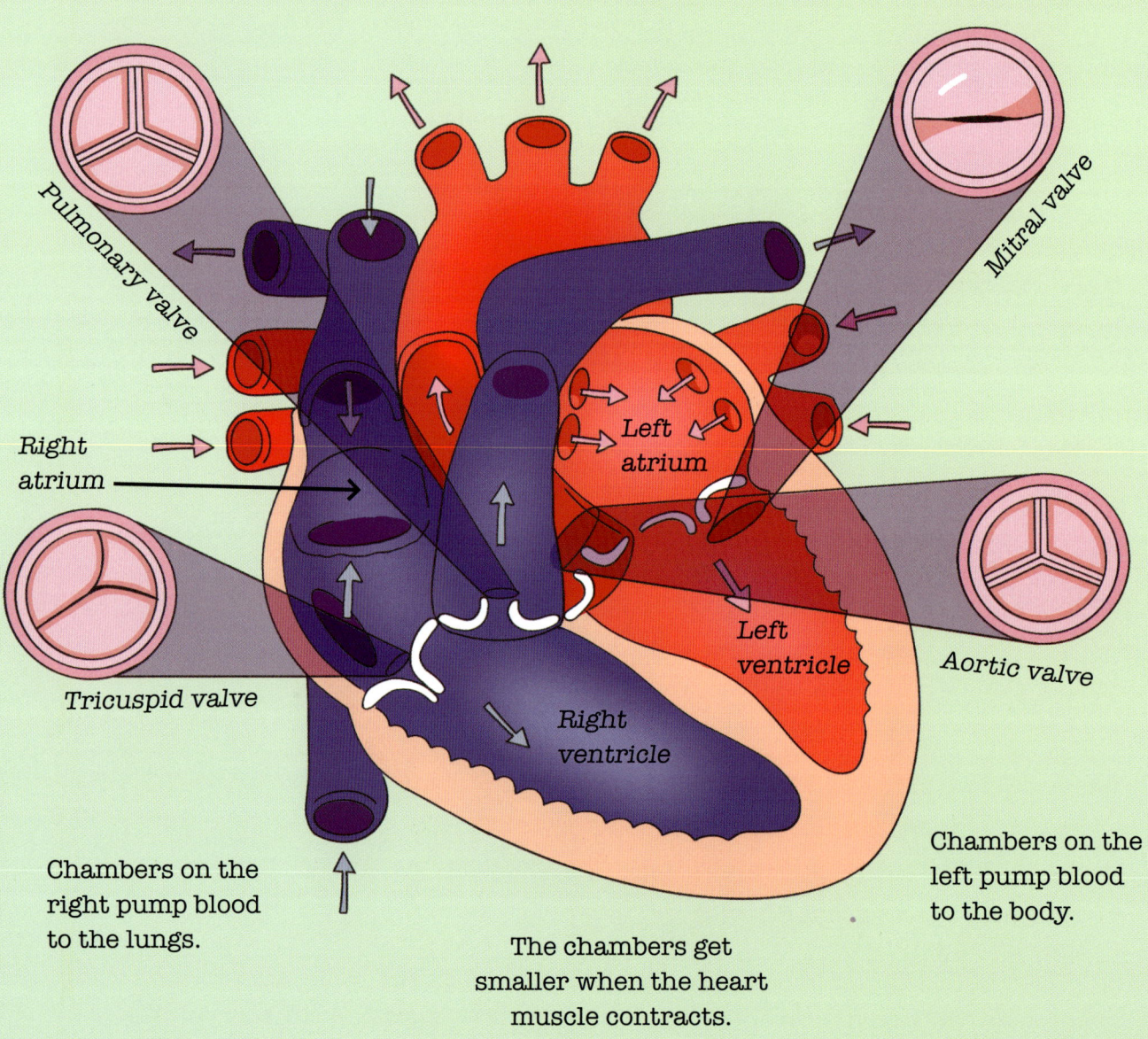

Pulmonary valve

Mitral valve

Right atrium

Left atrium

Tricuspid valve

Left ventricle

Aortic valve

Right ventricle

Chambers on the right pump blood to the lungs.

The chambers get smaller when the heart muscle contracts.

Chambers on the left pump blood to the body.

Made for Breathing

Protected by your rib cage are your two lungs. They fill most of the space inside your chest. The lungs are like two spongy bags that fill with air when you breathe in. They supply your body with the oxygen that it needs to work and get rid of waste carbon dioxide gas.

You breathe air in and out through your mouth and nose.

A pipe called the **TRACHEA** (or **WINDPIPE**) leads from your throat to your lungs.

A **BRONCHUS** leads to each lung.

The **LUNGS** are the main part of your respiratory system.

The **LEFT LUNG** is slightly smaller than the **RIGHT LUNG** and both can be broken up into parts, called **LOBES**. The left lung has two lobes. The right lung has three lobes.

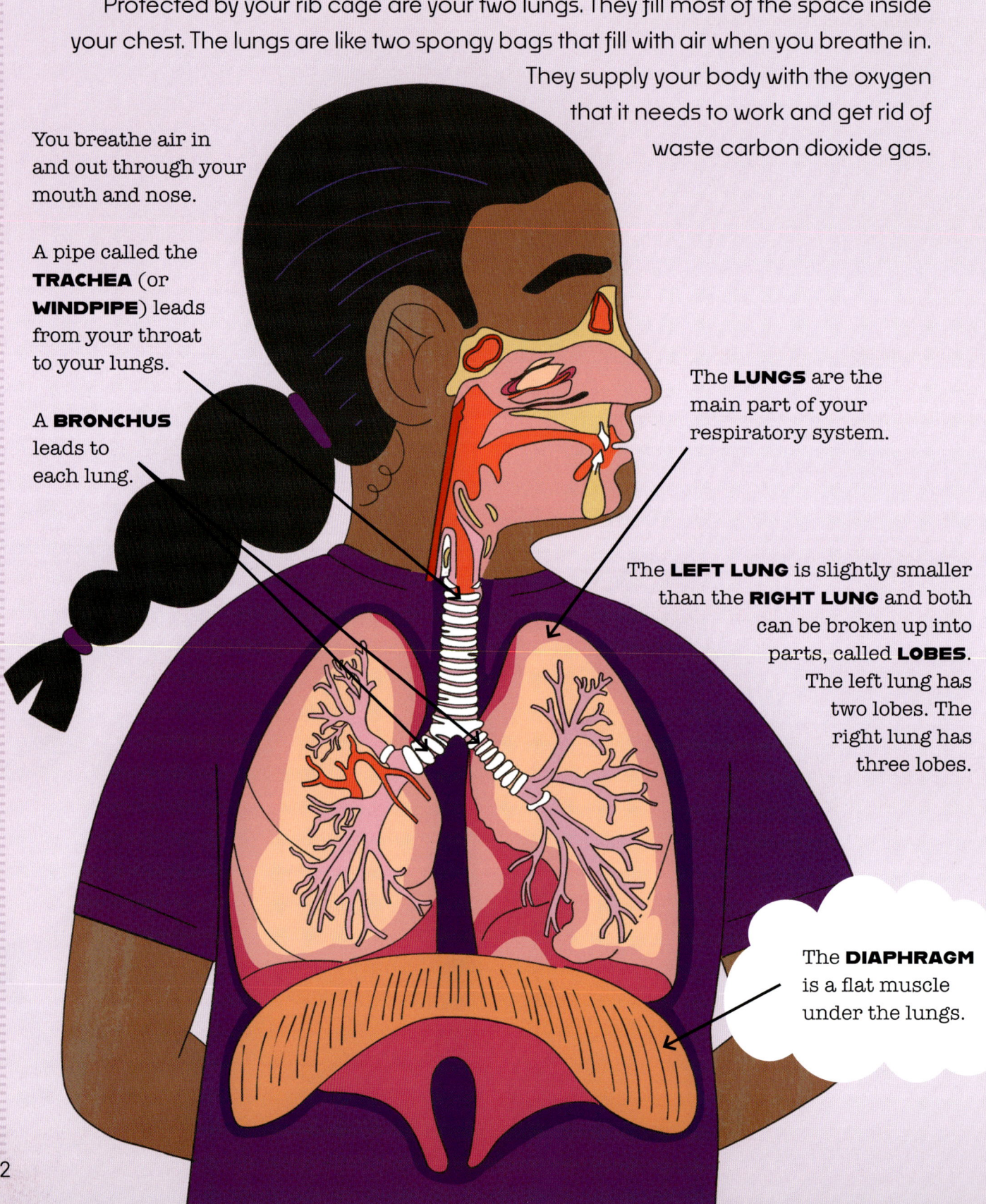

The **DIAPHRAGM** is a flat muscle under the lungs.

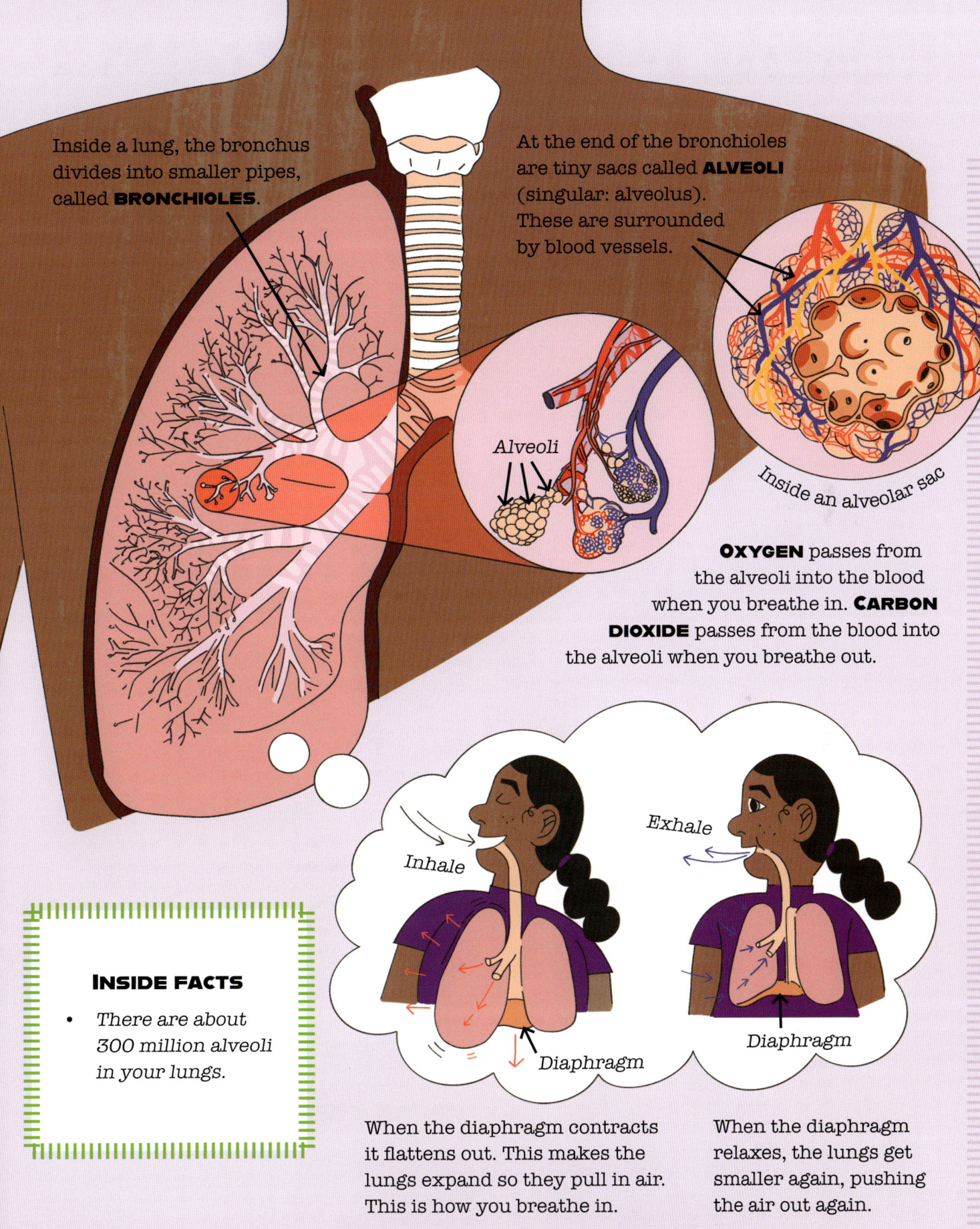

Inside a lung, the bronchus divides into smaller pipes, called **BRONCHIOLES**.

At the end of the bronchioles are tiny sacs called **ALVEOLI** (singular: alveolus). These are surrounded by blood vessels.

Alveoli

Inside an alveolar sac

OXYGEN passes from the alveoli into the blood when you breathe in. **CARBON DIOXIDE** passes from the blood into the alveoli when you breathe out.

Inhale *Exhale*

Diaphragm *Diaphragm*

When the diaphragm contracts it flattens out. This makes the lungs expand so they pull in air. This is how you breathe in.

When the diaphragm relaxes, the lungs get smaller again, pushing the air out again.

INSIDE FACTS
- There are about 300 million alveoli in your lungs.

DEALING WITH FOOD

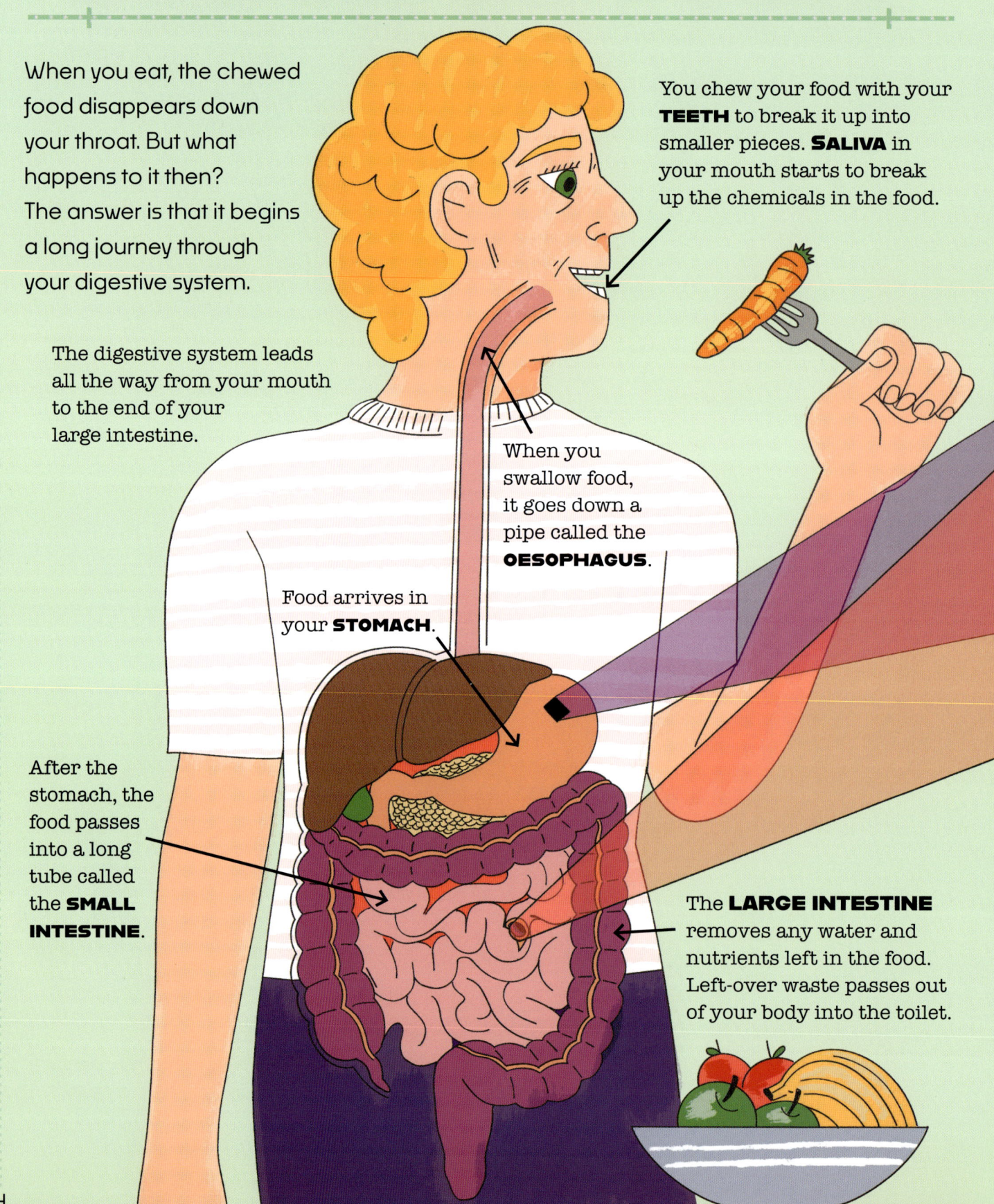

When you eat, the chewed food disappears down your throat. But what happens to it then? The answer is that it begins a long journey through your digestive system.

The digestive system leads all the way from your mouth to the end of your large intestine.

You chew your food with your **TEETH** to break it up into smaller pieces. **SALIVA** in your mouth starts to break up the chemicals in the food.

When you swallow food, it goes down a pipe called the **OESOPHAGUS**.

Food arrives in your **STOMACH**.

After the stomach, the food passes into a long tube called the **SMALL INTESTINE**.

The **LARGE INTESTINE** removes any water and nutrients left in the food. Left-over waste passes out of your body into the toilet.

The stomach's strong muscles churn the food. It mixes with a liquid called **GASTRIC JUICE**, which contains strong acid, and works to break the food up. This makes a thick liquid called **CHYME**.

ZOOM IN!

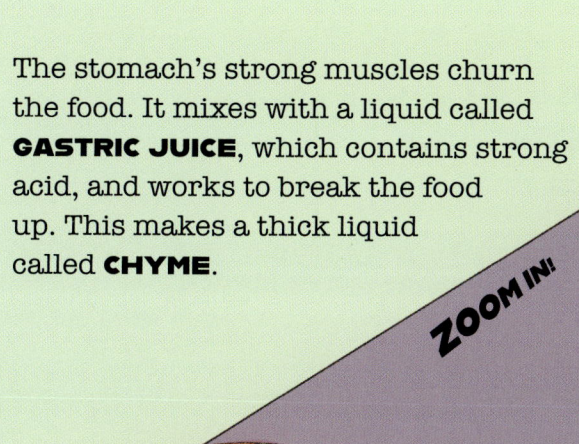

The stomach is a stretchy, expandable bag of many layers of muscle.

Villi

On the inside of the small intestine there are millions of tiny bumps called **VILLI**, which are surrounded by blood vessels. Via the villi, **NUTRIENTS** from food (carbohydrates, vitamins, fats and proteins) pass from the intestine into the blood.

The liver, kidneys and pancreas also help with digestion.

The **LIVER** stores nutrients from the digestive system, and makes chemicals called bile that your body needs.

Bean-shaped **KIDNEYS** remove waste from your blood to make urine, which it sends along to your bladder.

The **PANCREAS** makes digestive juices to help your stomach process sugars.

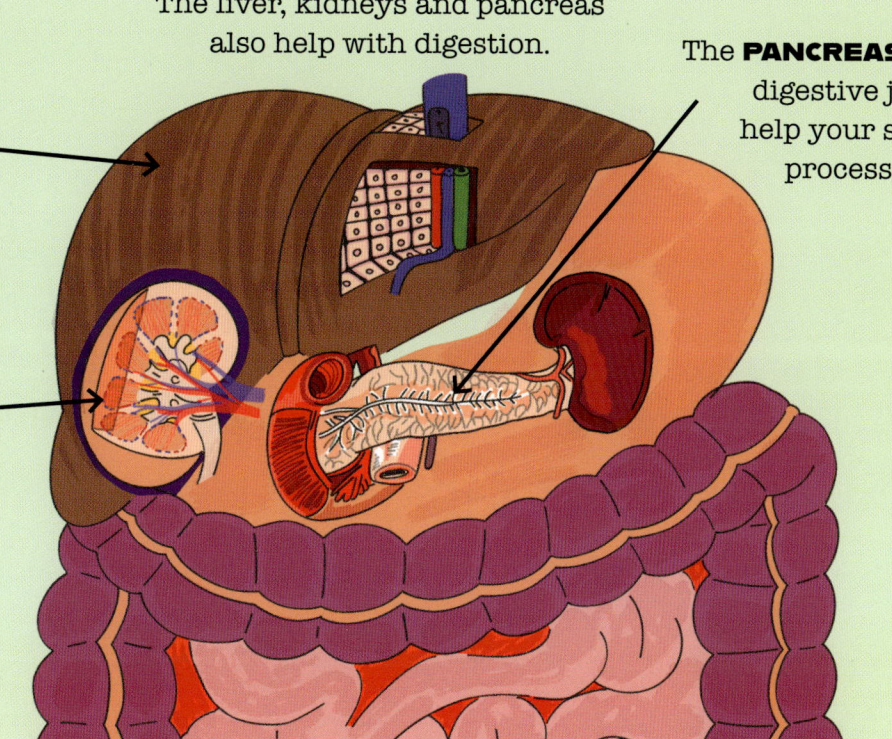

25

Body Building Blocks

Your whole body is made from cells – trillions and trillions of them. There are many different types of cell, each with its own shape and with its own job to do. Blood cells, skin cells, and nerve cells are just a few.

Cells are very tiny – too small to see with the naked eye. With a microscope you can see all the parts of a cell. This is the inside of a **SKIN CELL**.

CYTOPLASM is a jelly-like material that fills the cell.

The cell **MEMBRANE** is like a container for the cell. It holds the cell together. Chemicals such as oxygen can pass through the membrane to get in and out of the cell.

VACUOLES get rid of waste chemicals.

MITOCHONDRIA produce the energy the cell needs.

The **NUCLEUS** is the cell's control centre. Chemicals inside the nucleus called **CHROMOSOMES** tell the cell what to do.

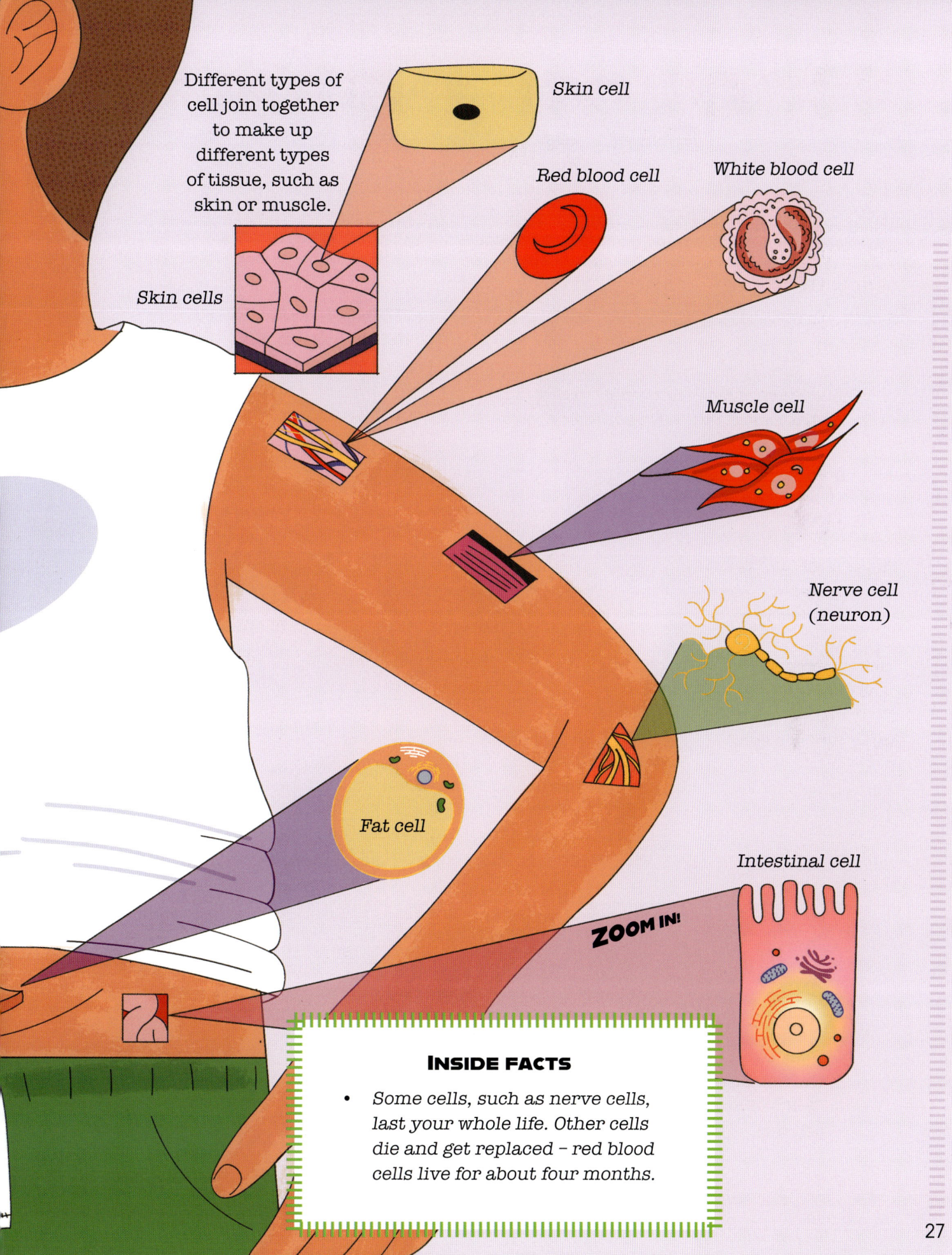

A Look Inside

In the past, doctors had to cut open a body to find out what was going on inside. Luckily, modern doctors have different medical instruments they use to examine your bones, tissues and organs if you are injured or ill.

ULTRASOUND is sound that's so high-pitched humans can't hear it. An ultrasound scanner sends ultrasound into the body. It detects echoes from the body and uses them to build a picture of what's inside.

Ultrasound is often used to examine **FOETUSES** to make sure they are developing healthfully before they are born.

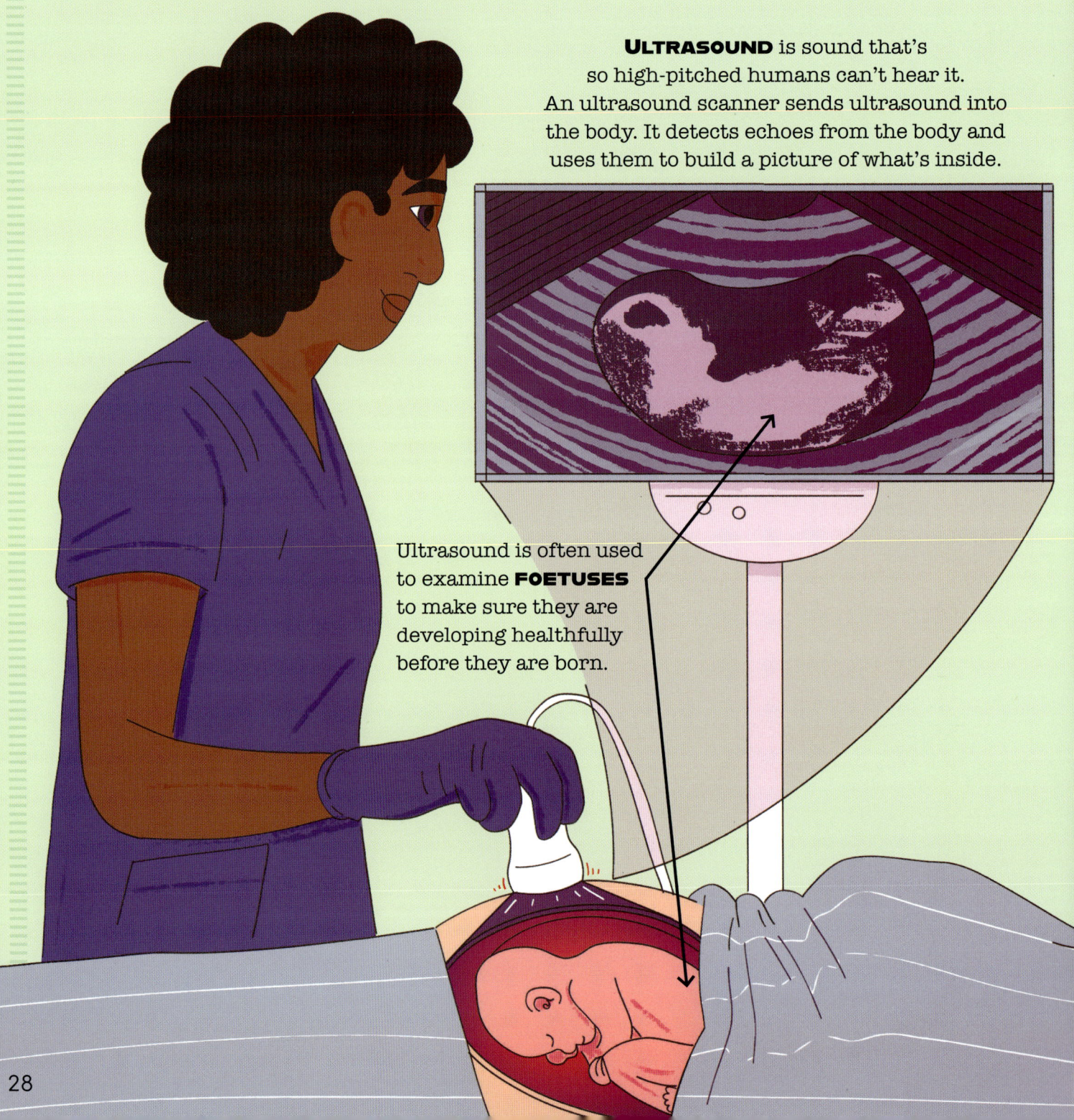

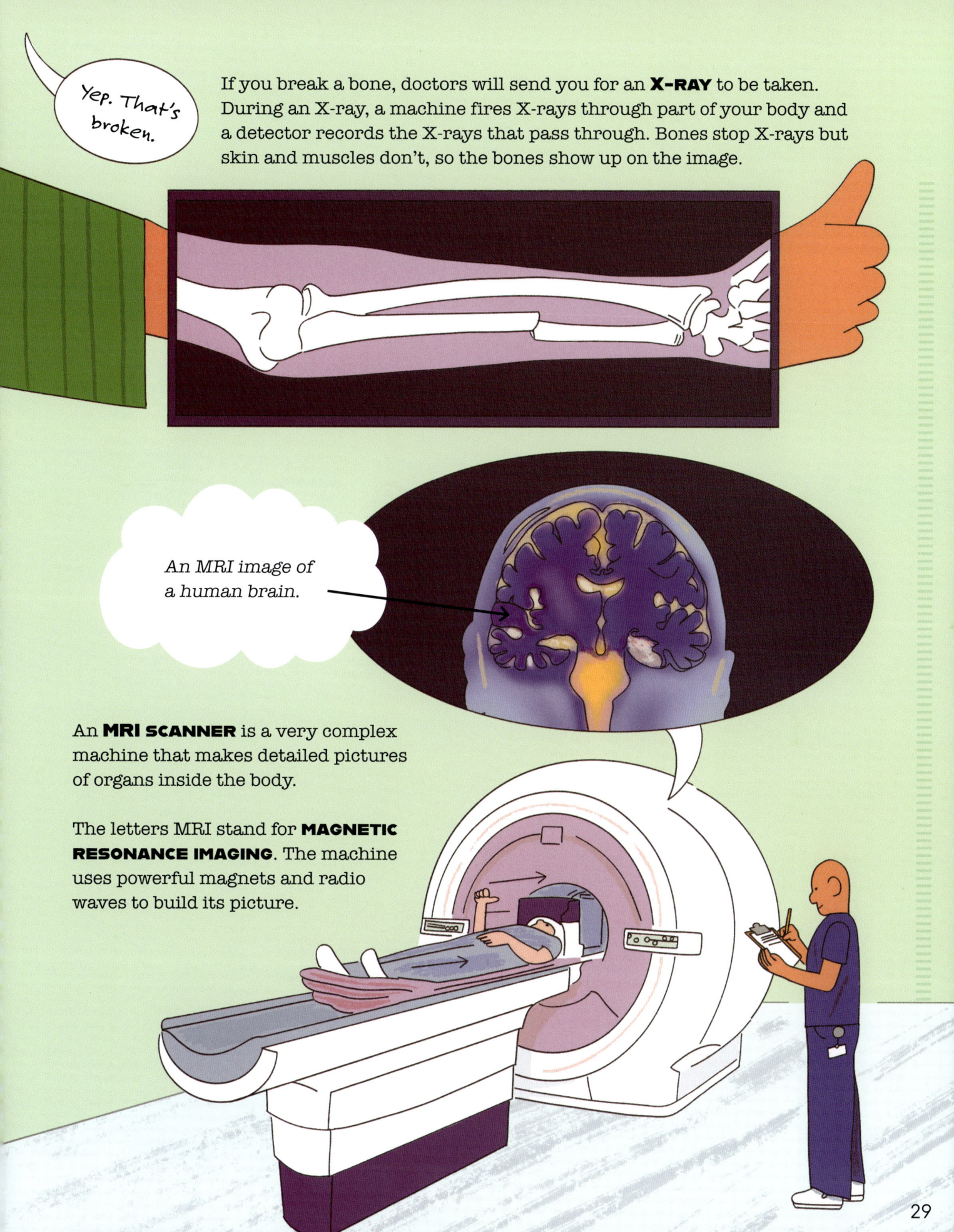

GLOSSARY

Blood The liquid that flows around your body, carrying chemicals that your cells need to live, carrying away waste chemicals, and carrying cells that fight disease and make repairs.

Blood vessel A pipe that carries blood around the body. Arteries, veins and capillaries are all blood vessels.

Cell One of the basic building blocks that make up your body. There are many different types of cell, such as red blood cells, nerve cells, and skin cells.

Circulatory system The parts of your body – made up of your heart and blood vessels – that move blood around your body.

Contract To get shorter.

Digestive system The parts of your body – including your stomach and intestines – that process your food and take nutrients from the food.

Fat A substance made up of cells called fat cells that your body uses to store energy.

Heart An organ in your body made of muscle that pumps blood. The heart is part of your circulatory system.

Nerve A part of the nervous system that carries messages to and from your brain.

Nervous system A system made up of your brain and nerves that reaches every part of your body, sending signals to your brain and getting signals from your brain.

Organ A part of the body that does a particular job, such as the brain, heart or liver.

Red blood cell A cell that's carried in the blood that carries oxygen around the body. Red blood cells give blood its colour.

Respiratory system The parts of your body – including your lungs – that take air into your body to get oxygen.

Skeleton A frame that supports your body and protects your organs, made up of more than 200 bones, connected by joints.

Skin The outer layer of your body that protects your body from germs, contains hairs, and contains sweat glands that help to keep your cool.

Spine A line of bones down your back that supports your head, shoulders, and ribs. It also protects the nerves that run down your back, called the spinal cord.

Tissue A type of material made of cells that makes up the body, such as the skin, bone, and muscles.

Valve Part of the heart or a blood vessel that lets blood flow one way but not the other.

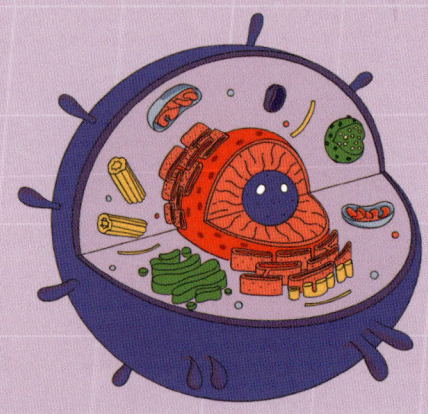

Further Information

More books to read:
Fact or Fake? The Truth About the Human Body by Izzi Howell
Wayland, 2022

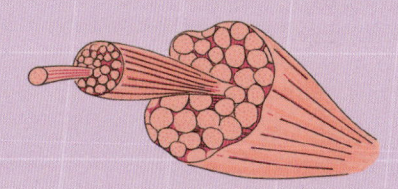

Funny Human Body Bits by Paul Mason
Wayland, 2025

What Matters Most?: Human Body Bits by Paul Mason
Wayland, 2024

Sites to visit:
www.bbc.co.uk/bitesize/topics/z7x78xs
Videos and quizzes from BBC Bitesize about different parts of the human body.

www.natgeokids.com/uk/category/discover/science/
The site from National Geographic Kids includes lots of interesting facts about the human body.

www.kidshealth.org/en/kids/center/htbw-main-page.html
Lots of fun videos and quizzes about the human body from the KidsHealth website.

Every effort has been made by the Publishers to ensure that the websites in this book are suitable for children, that they are of the highest educational value, and that they contain no inappropriate or offensive material. However, because of the nature of the internet, it is impossible to guarantee that the contents of these sites will not be altered. We strongly advise that internet access is supervised by a responsible adult.

INDEX

arteries 19, 21

blood 5, 6, 9, 13, 18-21, 23, 25, 26, 27
blood vessels 6, 9, 12, 18-21, 23, 25
bones 4, 9, 10-13, 19, 28, 29
breaks 13, 29
brain 5, 8, 10, 11, 14, 15, 16, 17, 29
breathing 14, 22-23

carbon dioxide 22, 23
cartilage 10
cells 6, 13, 14, 17, 18, 19, 26-27
    structure of 26
chemicals 4, 5, 19, 24, 25, 26
circulatory system 5, 18-21

diaphragm 22, 23
digestive system 4, 24-25
doctors 4, 28, 29

ears 17
eyes 14, 17

fat 6, 13, 25, 27
food 4, 15, 24-25

germs 6, 18

hair 6, 7
heart 5, 9, 10, 14, 18, 19, 20-21

intestines 4, 24, 25, 27

joints 4, 8, 11

kidneys 25

ligaments 11
liver 25
lungs 4, 10, 15, 18, 20, 21, 22-23

marrow 13
mouth 4, 14, 15, 24
MRI scanner 29
muscle 4, 5, 8-9, 10, 20, 21, 22, 25, 27, 29

nerves 7, 9, 12, 16-17, 26, 27
nervous system 5, 14, 16-17
nose 14, 15, 17
nutrients 24-25

organs 10, 14, 19, 28, 29
oxygen 4, 5, 18, 21, 22, 23, 26

plasma 18

respiratory system 4, 14, 22-23

senses 5, 7, 14, 16-17, 28
skeleton 4, 8, 10-11
skin 4, 5, 6-7, 8, 19, 26, 27, 29
skull 10, 14-15
spine 8, 10, 11, 16
stomach 4, 9, 24, 25
sweat 7

teeth 10, 14, 15
tendons 9

ultrasound scanner 28

valves 19, 20
veins 19, 20

waste, body 24, 25, 26

X-ray 29

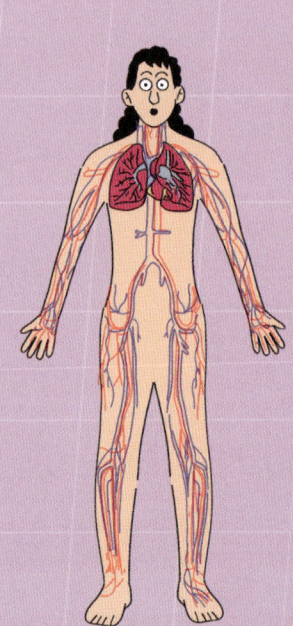